The Wonder of
OWLS

To Matthew, Maria, Emily, Tom, and Camille, with special thanks to Doris, Barb, and Leanne.

— Neal Niemuth

For a free color catalog describing Gareth Stevens Publishing's list of high-quality books and multimedia programs, call 1-800-542-2595 (USA) or 1-800-461-9120 (Canada). Gareth Stevens Publishing's Fax: (414) 332-3567.

Library of Congress Cataloging-in-Publication Data available upon request from publisher. Fax: (414) 332-3567 for the attention of the Publishing Records Department.

ISBN 0-8368-2664-7

First published in North America in 2000 by
Gareth Stevens Publishing
A World Almanac Education Group Company
330 West Olive Street, Suite 100
Milwaukee, WI 53212 USA

This edition is based on the book *Owls for Kids* © 1995 by Neal D. Niemuth, with illustrations by John F. McGee, first published in the United States in 1995 by NorthWord Press, Inc., Minocqua, Wisconsin, and published as *Owl Magic for Kids* in a library edition by Gareth Stevens, Inc., in 1996. Additional end matter © 2000 by Gareth Stevens, Inc.

Photographs © 1995: Dembinsky Photo Associates: Cover, 11, 13, 20, 23, 28, 33, 36-37, 40, 41, 44, 45; John Hendrickson: 12, 31, 34, 38, 46-47; Gerard Fuehrer: 14, 26; Rod Planck: 4, 6-7.

Printed in the United States of America

1 2 3 4 5 6 7 8 9 04 03 02 01 00

The Wonder of
OWLS

by Amy Bauman and Neal Niemuth
Illustrations by John F. McGee

Gareth Stevens Publishing
A WORLD ALMANAC EDUCATION GROUP COMPANY

No matter where you live, the chances are good that you will see an owl one day. Owls are large birds that live all over the world in all kinds of habitats.

With their broad, fluffy bodies, curved beaks, and large eyes, owls look very different from other birds.

snowy owl

The snowy owl is just one of the many kinds of owls that share our world. There are about 145 species, or types, of owls, and they come in many sizes.

snowy owl

The smallest owl is the elf owl. It stands about 6 inches (15 centimeters) tall. The largest owl is the great gray owl. It can grow to 30 inches (76 cm) tall. Snowy owls are about 20 inches (51 cm) tall. When owls spread their wings, they look bigger still!

Snowy owls usually live in the far north. Their favorite habitat is the Arctic tundra. The owl's white color makes it hard to spot in this treeless, snow-covered land.

Snowy owls are more active
during the day. Other owls
are more active at night.

Owls are excellent hunters.
They hunt insects, birds,
and small mammals, such
as mice and voles.

Owls go where they can find food. During some winters, snowy owls may fly south to find food. That is when people in the United States and Canada see them.

snowy owl

When snowy owls travel south,
they look for open, treeless
areas like their northern homes.
They land along lakeshores, in
fields — even at airports!

Owls can see very well, both during the day and at night. They have very big eyes for their small bodies. If people's eyes were as large for their bodies as owls' eyes, human eyes would be as big as oranges!

Owls cannot move their eyes around like people can. They have to turn their heads to look in a certain direction. Owls can turn their heads from side to side very quickly. Sometimes it looks as if they are spinning their heads all the way around!

The eyes of owls are well protected. Owls have two sets of eyelids. Like people, they have a pair of solid eyelids. They also have see-through eyelids — like built-in goggles! As an owl flies around trees or swoops down on prey, its see-through eyelids close to provide extra protection.

snowy owl

Owls hear very well, too. Soft feathers hide small ear flaps on each side of their heads. Disc-shaped feathers on an owl's face funnel sound into its ears.

Some owls have tufts on their heads that look like ears, but they are really just feathers. They don't help owls hear at all.

great horned owl

Owls hear so well that they can catch prey without even seeing it. Owls find mice under the snow by listening to them run.

Some people call owls "mousetraps with wings." A single barn owl can catch as many as 11,000 mice in its lifetime!

snowy owl

Owls are hunters from head to toe. They use their sharp talons to catch and carry prey.

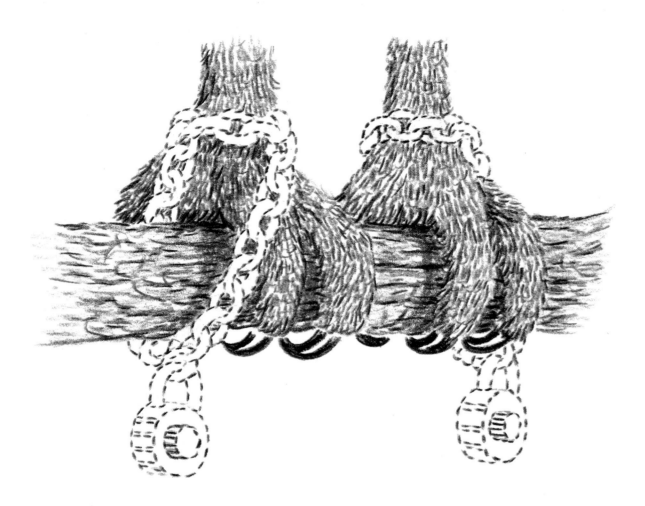

As an owl sits, looking and listening for prey, its toes can lock into position so it won't fall off its perch.

Owls do not have teeth, so they cannot chew their food. They will often swallow their prey whole — bones, fur, and all!

barn owl

Several hours after owls eat, they cough up pellets. The pellets contain parts of prey, such as bones and fur, that owls cannot digest.

Unlike most other birds, owls do not build their own nests. Some owls will use old nests made by hawks or crows. Others make homes in hollow trees, on rocky ledges, or even in holes in the ground.

barn owl

The nests
of owls
have to
be very
strong.
An owl's
home
must be
a safe
place for
laying
eggs and
raising
young.

Many owls lay their eggs in early spring. Then the babies have all summer to grow and learn how to fly and hunt for themselves.

great horned owl

great horned owls

Once a female owl lays eggs, she rarely leaves the nest. While she sits on the eggs, the male flies off to hunt.

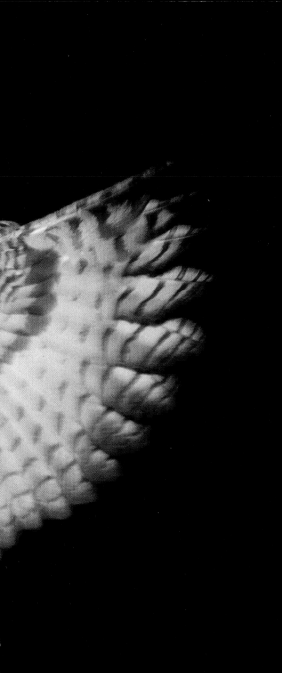

Owls fly very quietly. The shape and softness of their feathers keep their wings from making noise as they fly. It is easier for owls to hear prey when their wings don't make noise.

great horned owl

A male owl does all the hunting until the eggs hatch. Then both parents have to hunt — they have more mouths to feed! Both male and female owls care for their young.

great horned owl

eastern screech owl

How soon the eggs will hatch depends on the size of the eggs.

saw-whet owl

Small eggs need about 21 days to hatch. Large eggs hatch in about 35 days. Small owls, such as saw-whet owls, lay eggs that are the size of big marbles. Great horned owls lay eggs that are the size of chicken eggs.

An owl might not lay all of her eggs at once. Often, she lays only one egg and sits on it for a day or two. Then she lays another egg.

Owl parents are protective of their nests. An owl will stand up straight and spread its wings to scare away unwelcome visitors!

Young owls have thick, fuzzy feathers. Little owls are ready to leave the nest in just a few weeks.

great gray owls

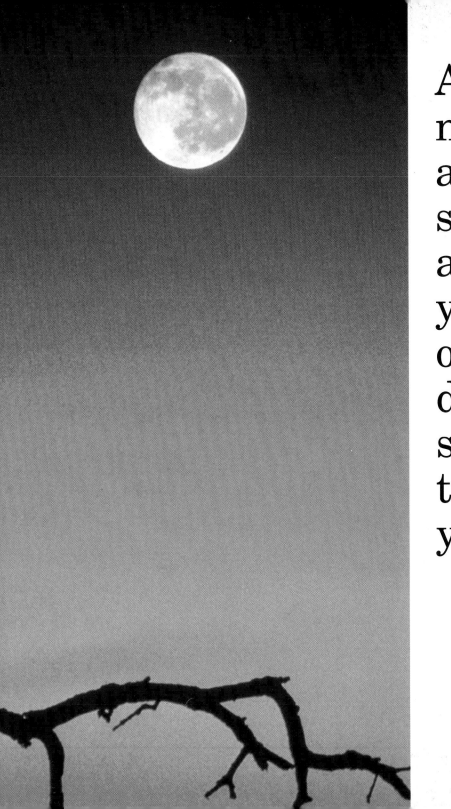

An owl at night is an awesome sight. If you are lucky, you will see one — but don't be surprised if the owl sees you first!

Glossary

digest – to break down and absorb food after it is eaten

habitats – the places where animals and plants live in nature

mammals – animals with hair or fur that feed their young with mother's milk

pellets – balls of undigested food that owls cough up after eating

perch – (n) a spot, such as a branch or pole, where birds sit or rest

prey – animals that are hunted by other animals for food

talons – long, sharp claws found on the feet of birds that hunt

tufts – clusters of feathers on some owls' heads, that often look like ears

tundra – the flat, treeless land often found in arctic areas

voles – small rodents, similar to mice but with shorter legs and tails

Index